The Hamlyn
Book of
Skateboarding

The Hamlyn Book of Skateboarding

Peter Arnold

with technical advice by courtesy of
Beadle Products Limited

Special photography by John Howard

Hamlyn
London · New York · Sydney · Toronto

The publishers would like to express their appreciation for the assistance given by the following during the preparation of this book:

David Gower
The Beadle Skateboard Team
(Ki Gerhardt, Paul Kambur, David Sogan, Sebastian Witkin)
Skatecity
The British Red Cross Society
The British Safety Council
The St Andrew Ambulance Association
The St John Ambulance Association

and to the following for providing photographs:

All-Sport
Alpine Sport
David Gower
Skateboard Special
Tony Stone Associates
Topix
Zefa

Illustrated by Bob Mathias and James Val

First published 1977
Fifth impression 1978
The Hamlyn Publishing Group Limited London / New York / Sydney / Toronto
Astronaut House, Feltham, Middlesex, England.

ISBN 0 600 38302 4

Printed in Italy

Contents

About skateboarding

Skateboarding offers the same excitement as surfing and skiing. It has an advantage over these sports, however, because it can be enjoyed by those who have no access to surf beaches or snow-covered slopes. It is an urban sport, offering an exhilarating mixture of speed, skill and fun.

Surfing is the direct ancestor of skateboarding, and early skateboards were made from surfboards.

The chances are, though, that parents will take a different view. So far as many are concerned, a skateboard and its rider are an alarming combination of speed and danger! Nobody taking up skateboarding can help falling once in a while, and concrete and asphalt are hard. Cuts and bruises are a part of growing up, but even the most sympathetic parent, thinking that there is the slightest chance of something like a broken limb, might say the risk is too great. Many sports have an element of danger, but it is easy to understand why parents think skateboarding is *too* dangerous.

There is another objection to skateboarding, which might be raised by the public at large, not only by the parents of skateboarders. A boy or girl skateboarding in and out of traffic on a road, or weaving between pedestrians in a shopping precinct, is a danger not only to himself or herself but to everyone.

Where does the truth lie concerning the risks of skateboarding? Well, obviously, if the author and publishers of this book thought that skateboarding is *necessarily* too dangerous, then this book would not be produced. Skateboarding is an exciting sport, which shares with other physical activities the need for those who practise it to take a responsible attitude towards safety. Provided they do, there should be no serious injuries.

Skateboarding is in some ways like riding a bicycle or swimming. It is a skill that, once learned, comes naturally and is not forgotten. The similarity with cycling and swimming continues after the art is learned. With each of the three sports, learning how to do it does not mean you can forget about safety. Indeed you have to think harder about it. And safety includes what to wear and where to practise the sport.

In Britain the British Safety Council has already issued a safety code, which is included here. It is a very important part of the book. The young skateboarder, who perhaps acquires this book with his first skateboard, will be anxious to get out and start. He or she might well think that safety is common sense, and that this section can be skipped. Nothing could be sillier. It does not take long to read the section on safety. When you've read this book, read the safety section again, and remember that all the points mentioned are made for *your* benefit, and by observing them you could save yourself from an accident.

The aim of this book is to help the reader to become a good, *safe* skateboarder. Advice includes what to look for when buying a board, how to begin, how to acquire the various techniques of downhill, slalom, and free-style riding – with tricks to do when you acquire skill – and how to look after your skateboard. To put it all into perspective, we begin with a page on the history and development of the sport.

Good luck, and good skateboarding!

How it began

Some people do not consider skateboarding as a modern sport and some writers, when discussing the beginnings of skateboarding, go back several thousand years to the invention of the wheel. Certainly somebody in the dim and distant past must have hit upon the idea of putting small wheels under a board and riding it downhill, but who is to say who it was or when it happened first.

Roller-skates were invented in the eighteenth century, and they must have led to many early skateboarders. It is not difficult to imagine an ingenious boy attaching the wheels of a broken roller-skate to a piece of wood and making a primitive skateboard. The clay roller-skate wheels which were made during the first half of this century were useful for all sorts of purposes, and made good scooters as well as rudimentary skateboards. Roller-skating is not really an ancestor of modern

Ready made wheels were roller-skating's early contribution to skateboarding.

skateboarding, however, and if you are thinking of making yourself a cheap skateboard from an old pair of roller-skates, please forget it! You will discover from the section on skateboards that your home-made board will not be satisfactory, and you will very soon become disappointed with its limitations. Skateboarding uses a different technique to roller-skating, although it is true that the technology learned from skateboarding has led to improvements in roller-skates. Skateboarding is closer to surfing and skiing, where there are no wheels at all, but where the sportsman uses his balance and body movements to glide over the waves or the snow.

It is difficult even to go back only twenty or so years and say exactly when *modern* skateboarding began. In the 1950s and early 1960s the popular sport of surfing was enjoying a boom on the west coast of California. From this boom arose a 'pop' culture which inspired millions of young people. In the early 1960s pop groups like The Beach Boys were helping to bring the way of life of the Californian west coast to the attention of the rest of the world. This way of life centred around the sun, the beaches and surfing. The Californian surfing community was the first to develop the idea that some of the excitement of surfing could be obtained on land, by using roller-skate wheels attached to short surf boards. It was because so many people were making skateboards from roller-skates (even though they were not very satisfactory) that a surfboard manufacturer first asked a roller-skate manufacturer about the possibility of supplying trucks and wheels (ie the complete wheel assembly) to which high-quality boards could be added to make skateboards. Eventually, around 1962, skateboards were in production. They were not very good by today's standards, but millions were bought with enthusiasm, and skateboarding very rapidly changed in status from a passing craze to a sport.

Even so, it would not be quite true to say that modern skateboarding started even then, because in a couple of years skateboarding was virtually dead. It died for two reasons. First, it became a nuisance, and when statistics in a California Medical Association report highlighted the accident rate, cities in America took the opportunity to ban it from the streets.

That the public disliked skateboarding was, however, less important than that skateboarders themselves lost interest. This was because the skateboards were not very efficient. Being based on the roller-skate wheels then available, they were noisy and not nearly as manoeuvrable as they are today. The heavier wear that skateboards put upon the wheels led to the wheels wearing out in no time at all. By 1966 skateboarding looked to have gone the way of other fads like yo-yos and hula-hoops. As soon as everybody could perform all that was possible with them, they rapidly lost interest.

That was where skateboarding might have ended. But around 1973 polyurethane wheels were tried on skateboards. They made skateboards quicker, more manoeuvrable, and therefore safer. Suddenly, all sorts of new, exciting tricks could be performed on skateboards. To the faithful few who had remained true to the sport, it seemed like a dream come true. Then more thought was given to the composition of the deck. The modern skateboard, with its specially designed deck, truck and polyurethane wheels, is a very different article to the skateboard of the 1960s.

The boom began all over again. This time it was better founded. Learning from earlier mistakes, skateboarders are now more considerate of the rest of the public and more concerned for the safety of themselves and others. Specially designed protective clothing and helmets are being manufactured.

Beginning in America, modern skateboarding spread in the 1970s to other parts of the world. America still leads, of course, with many specially designed or adapted skateboard parks, and proliferating competitions. The international magazine *Skateboarder*, with a reported circulation of over 200,000 copies per issue, is published there.

In Britain, skateboarding is very new, beginning only in 1976. But development is fast. With the American experience as a guide, mistakes can be avoided, and in all ways skateboarding is more sophisticated in Britain than it was at the same stage of its development in America. In 1977 there were already a number of skateboard parks operating and at least four skateboard magazines competing with each other in an attempt to become the best-selling magazine of Great Britain.

Will the current boom in America and Britain survive and spread to other countries? Well, that depends mostly on the skateboarder, and that is *you*. Modern skateboarding can be said to have really taken off in the 1970s. You are part of a new sport. If you show consideration to the rest of the public, and follow all the safety rules so that you do not get involved in accidents, then you could be among the first to practise what could become one of the world's leading sports.

Skiers share with skateboarders the joys of the downhill run and the slalom.

Into gear

The first thing the prospective skateboarder must do is obtain a board. This is not as straightforward as it sounds. A big selection is available, covering a wide price range. It is easy to spend your available money on a board with which you will later be disappointed, and taking your

time to find the right board, perhaps even deferring purchase until you've saved more money and can buy the board you really want, is well worth it.

Choosing a board

Anybody who reads a book like this, which attempts to introduce the reader to a sport, will find a chapter on buying equipment, and the advice always seems to be the same; buy the best you can afford. It is easy to take this advice with a pinch of salt. If you are learning angling, for example, you might think that a cheap rod catches fish just as an expensive rod does. It might not do it so well, but it is basically a less efficient model of the same thing, and quite adequate to learn on. It would be wrong to think of skateboards in the same way. From the previous section on history, you will have learned how skateboarding faded in the 1960s because the skateboards were inferior.

You can apply this knowledge when buying a skateboard. The cheapest might be fine, if all you want to do is rattle downhill on a gentle slope and stop at the bottom. However, after a while you will want to progress to more exciting moves, and eventually you will want to try some of the free-style manoeuvres described later. Unfortunately, if you buy a very cheap skateboard, you will then find that it will not allow you to do them. It is not designed for clever tricks. You may then decide, wrongly, that the sport is too difficult for you and give it up, or alternatively you will be forced to sell your board and buy a better one, which will involve you in extra expense.

You will realize then, that a cheap skateboard is not even just an inferior version of a good, expensive skateboard. It actually prevents you doing many of the things you might want to do.

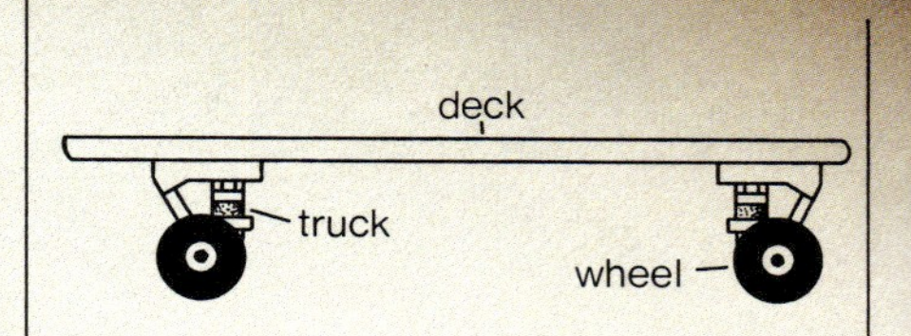

Before we consider the type of skateboard you might expect to buy for your money, let us look at what makes up a skateboard. There are three main parts: the deck, the truck and the wheels.

Decks

Most decks (sometimes called boards, but we will reserve this term for the whole skateboard) are made of one of these materials: plywood, rigid fibreglass, hardwood, polypropylene, polyvinyl chloride (pvc), polycarbonate, aluminium, fibreglass, or a fibreglass and hardwood laminate.

When you buy a board, you should consider the shape, appearance, 'feel' and durability of your deck. Shape is a matter of personal choice. Most decks are shaped like a boat, more pointed at the front than the back. However, the nose takes a certain amount of battering from time to time, and should therefore be gently rounded rather than pointed or with corners. Kick-tails,

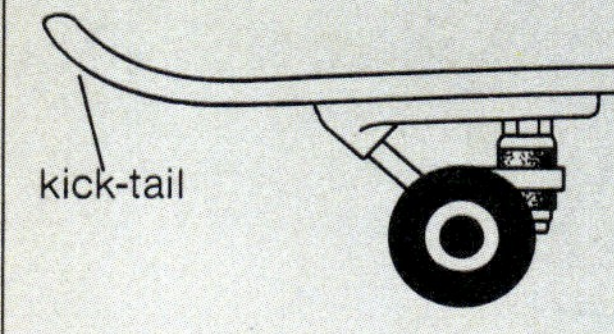

kick-noses and cambers are common, and as well as looking good they help in some of the free-style tricks. Other fancy tails and noses, like swallow tails, do nothing for performance, and unless you have a particular liking for one it is best to choose the gently rounded standard shape.

Would-be champions cannot begin too early and this young rider already has the correct gear to aim high.

The 'feel' of the deck is the most important point to consider. Basically there are two types of 'feel' – rigid or flexible. Generally a rigid deck is preferred for tricks as it transmits the torque

A most desirable possession for the keen skateboarder—a top flight board of wood and fibreglass laminate.

generated by the body directly through the skateboard. For example, when you depress the end of the skateboard in order to lever the opposite end up you do not want to use part of that energy in bending a flexible deck. On the other hand, a flexible deck is preferred by those who go for speed and slalom, as the flexibility in the skateboard gives a smoother ride, thereby absorbing the vibration created at high speed more effectively.

A good flexible deck must possess the quality of 'memory'. Memory is the ability of the deck to resume its original shape at a quicker rate than it will deform. Cheap fibreglass and polypropylene products do not possess this ability and should best be regarded as durable rigid decks. The very best memory is undoubtedly possessed by a deck constructed with a fibreglass and hardwood lamination. These decks, however, are particularly expensive and in Britain it is not unusual to pay in excess of £25 for the deck alone. Good-quality fibreglass decks generally attain an acceptable memory level at about a third of the cost of a laminated deck.

The way to test a deck for flexibility is to stand between the wheels and make little jumps. If a deck is saggy, it will give but be slow to spring back. A good flexible deck might give by between 12 and 20mm (½ to ¾inch) and instantly return to its original position. You must decide yourself how much flexibility you like.

Let us consider now the properties of each type of deck construction.

Plywood is rigid, relatively strong, light in weight and inexpensive. It has the disadvantage that it can break suddenly, especially when you attempt tricks which involve creating substantial force in the centre of the board.

Rigid fibreglass has good 'cosmetic' properties, which means that a rigid fibreglass deck is colourful and has a good manufactured appearance. It is not as rigid as plywood and you should test its rigidity before purchase. It is light. It has the disadvantage that it can break without warning, although this is rare. It chips on impact.

Hardwood decks must be of a hard wood like oak or mahogany. The grain must run the length of the deck, without curving away at the edges, and if you are offered a deck with knots, reject it. Knots are for sailors, not skateboarders. A hardwood deck is absolutely rigid, and usually has a good kick-tail. Because it does not absorb the torque it is good for tricks. It has an attractive appearance, and because you cannot generally buy a hardwood deck for less than about £9 it is well finished and presented. It is relatively heavy. Some hardwoods suffer from 'shakes', which are minute fractures within the timber fibre caused by constant impact over a period of time, and which eventually lead to a split in the wood. Impact will create rough edges resulting in nasty splinters unless the edges are kept well sanded.

Polypropylene is extremely durable. It is unaffected by burns or chemicals and should last centuries, which should be long enough for you to hand over your deck to your children. Polypropylene decks are colourful and of good manufactured appearance, sometimes incorporating kick-tails or kick-noses. They are relatively cheap and probably the best beginner's deck for those who cannot afford a quality deck. There are disadvantages, however. It is impossible to obtain a suitable non-slip surface with polypropylene, and grip tape (which can be stuck on some decks to get a non-slip surface) will not stick to it either. Also, polypropylene is neither rigid nor flexible, and it has poor memory.

Polyvinyl chloride (pvc) decks are generally recognized by being translucent (in other words light will pass through them) and they possess relatively good cosmetic and flex qualities. They should be avoided for long term use as they suffer from fatigue and eventually break.

Polycarbonate decks are rare. They possess the same cosmetic and flexible qualities as pvc without the disadvantage of suffering from fatigue, but they are very expensive.

Aluminium decks possess relatively good cosmetic and flex properties but suffer from fatigue. They have the added disadvantage of developing razor sharp edges through wear. You might get the occasional close shave on your skateboard, but you will not want the sort a sharp aluminium deck could give you. Such a skateboard on a free run (ie travelling without a rider) is a lethal projectile.

Fibreglass of good quality makes decks of good flex and memory properties. They are cosmetically attractive. If produced from a mould they will have a good grip top, and in any case grip tape readily adheres to the surface. They are quite durable and they do not suffer from fatigue. Their disadvantage is that they chip, but they probably represent the best all-round value for money.

Fibreglass and hardwood laminate decks have tremendous flex and memory. They are quite durable and have excellent appearance. Grip tape sticks and is normally supplied as standard. You can regard these decks as the 'Formula 1' of skateboard decks. Beware imitations; inferior-quality versions are available. The only disadvantage of the genuine article is that it is very expensive and consequently highly desired by thieves.

Decks might be found in other materials, but so far they have not been manufactured in any quantity.

The average size skateboard is around 56 to 60cm (22 to 24inches) long, and 15cm (6inches) wide, slimmer at its rounded front than at the back. They can be obtained longer (even up to twice the normal length) and wider. Generally, the shorter the board, the better the manoeuvrability. A long board is best for speed, but a new skateboarder will find that the speed which can be generated on a standard-sized board will be sufficient.

Trucks

The truck is the assembly which is bolted or riveted to the underside of the board, and which houses the axle. On the best skateboards the truck helps in mobility and in absorbing shock. Cheaper skateboards might have trucks based on the roller-skate principle with one action pad between the board and the axle, as illustrated.

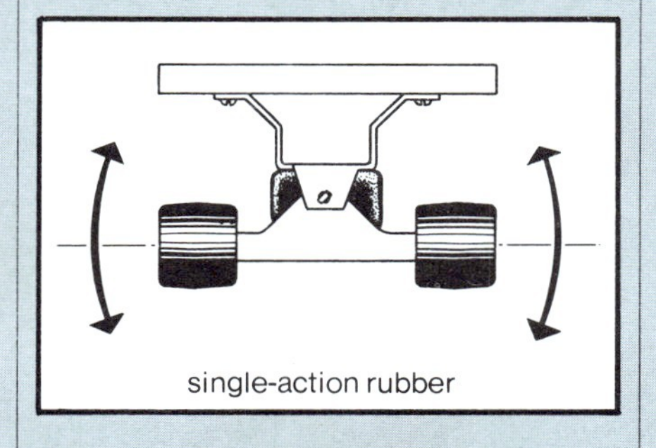
single-action rubber

This is sometimes called a single-action truck, and manoeuvrability is restricted to a side-to-side action. The best skateboards use two softer action

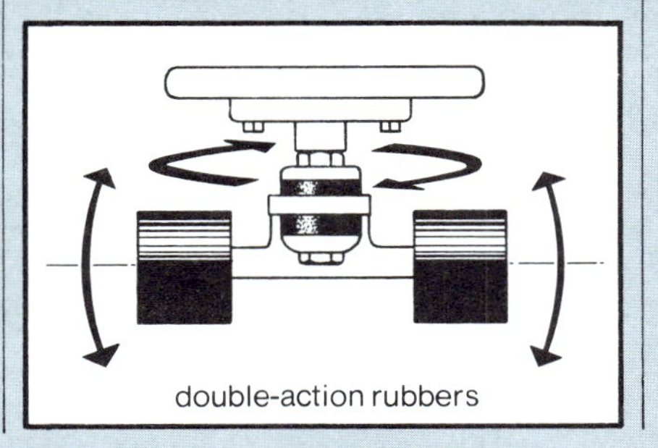
double-action rubbers

pads which give a double action. The principle is shown in the illustration.

Trucks are usually made of aluminium, and must be of a height to take the size of the wheel to be used. A truck which is too short will cause the wheel to rub against the deck when turning. The action bolt should not be lower than the axle housing. If it is, it might touch the ground in certain manoeuvres. A pad between the base plate and the deck will absorb shock but reduce the contact between you and the wheels and lessen your control. The fixing of pads should be considered carefully.

In general, if you are looking for the best truck, make sure that it has all the parts shown in the illustration on page 20.

Wheels

Wheels on skateboards began as roller-skate wheels, and were of clay composition. They were not suitable for skateboards because they were very hard. Traction (ie their grip of the ground) was poor, and on an uneven surface they were unreliable. Skateboard wheels should be soft for good traction. The cheapest skateboards will have rubber wheels, and the best will have polyurethane wheels.

Wheels will vary in hardness. The harder the wheel, the greater the speed it will achieve but the less its traction (grip) will be. Do not opt for a hard wheel just because you fancy skateboarding at great speed. The difference is only significant if you intend to enter the world speed championships. A wheel should have a good 'feel'. Squash the edge between your thumb and finger. There will be some 'give' but the wheel should quickly re-form its shape.

So far as the bearings in the wheel are concerned, wheels are of two types. The commoner is the *loose-bearing* wheel. This has

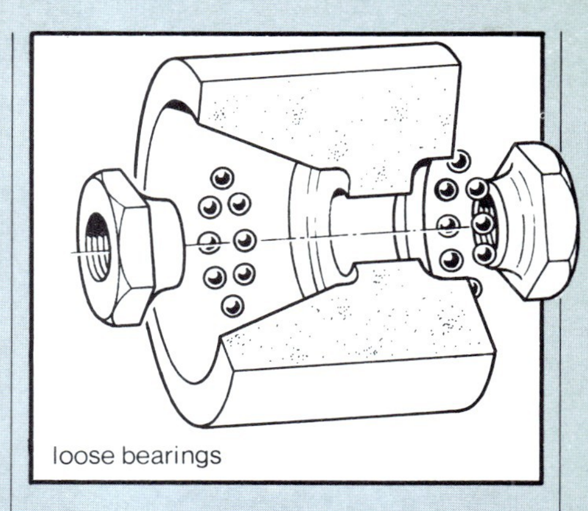
loose bearings

disadvantages. The bearings might, being loose, fall out of the wheel. This is rare, however. The wheel is noisier and gives a rougher ride. Also, dirt gets into the races (the part of the wheel in which the bearings run) and causes rapid wear. To keep it efficient the wheel must be regularly taken apart and cleaned. *Precision bearings* are set in the disc of the wheel, and are usually

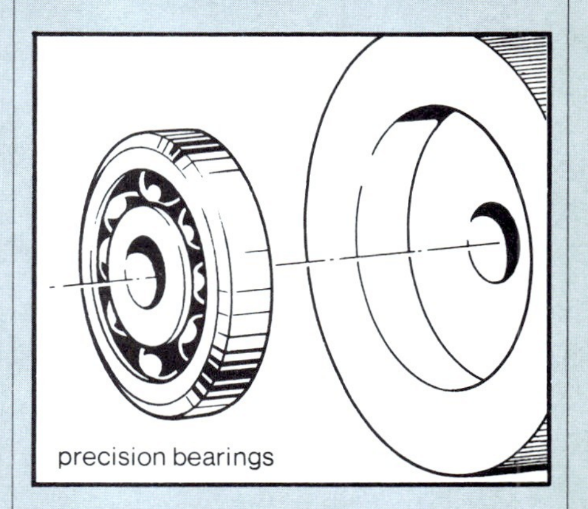
precision bearings

fully sealed. Precision-bearing wheels require no maintenance, but are much more expensive than loose-bearing wheels.

The width and diameter of the wheels are important. A standard wheel is about 30–32mm (1¼ inches) in width and about 50mm (2 inches) in diameter. A wider wheel of about 50mm (2 inches) width provides better traction and a smoother ride over rough ground. A wheel of about 75mm (3 inches) in width will give even more improved traction but possibly reduced manoeuvrability. The axle must be sufficient to take such wheels.

A word about brakes. Some cheap skateboards will have a big rubber pad on the back, the intention being that to stop, you turn the board up at the front so that the pad makes contact with the ground. Avoid boards with these brakes. Such pads are not only a poor way of stopping, they inhibit free-style riding. Stopping is best achieved by losing momentum when turning back uphill the way you came.

Types of skateboard

Illustrated in this section are four typical skateboards, one from each of four distinct price ranges. Number 1, shown in the centre here, is a top-flight skateboard, costing around £60 in Britain. It has a deck length of about 75cm (29–30 inches), high-quality aluminium trucks, and 75mm (3 inches) wide wheels with precision bearings. The wheels are of polyurethane, and the deck is of laminated wood and fibreglass. On this board you have flexibility, speed and good traction. As stated, it represents the Formula 1 in skateboarding.

Number 2 skateboard is the cheapest, usually known among skateboarders as a 'super cheapo'. In Britain it should cost no more than £8. The deck is about 50cm (20 inches) long and is made of plywood. It has single-action trucks. The wheels are loose-bearing rubber wheels of about 30mm (1¼ inches) width. As explained earlier, there is a limit to what can be performed on this board. There is no point in trying to improve it. None of its parts can be replaced with better-quality parts to improve performance. The whole will remain inadequate except for the most straightforward skateboarding. It is believed that four out of five people who buy skateboards of this type eventually give up the sport without going further. Most of the one in five who go on to better things miss out skateboards in the next price range and replace their 'super cheapo' with the fourth board described here.

Number 3 skateboard is in the price range above the super cheapo, and in Britain costs around £13 to £15. The deck is about 55–60cm (22–24 inches) long and made of polypropylene or rigid glassfibre. This gives more 'feel' than the super cheapo, but not true flexibility. The trucks are improved, with a wider axle width of around 10cm (4 inches) and are usually of the double-action type. The wheels are of cheap polyurethane or pvc, which are better than rubber roller-skate wheels but still lack the qualities of good polyurethane, and the loose bearings require constant and thorough maintenance and oiling. This board has scope for later improvement by changing the wheels and possibly the trucks to obtain better performance.

Number 4 skateboard illustrated costs around £25 in Britain. It has a good flexible deck of laminated fibreglass, 68–70cm (27 inches) long, which does not fatigue and has a good 'memory'. It has a non-slip surface and is cosmetically attractive: the board illustrated has camber and a kick-tail. The truck is of strong, high-quality aluminium. The wheels have precision bearings and are of good-quality polyurethane, with a width of about 50mm (2 inches). On this skateboard everything is changeable. You can fit the most expensive deck to your trucks, improve your trucks, or fit better wheels, and each change will give you an increased performance. If you are really keen on skateboarding it is better to save up for this model rather than experiment with a super cheapo, which you will find sooner or later you will have to change if you want to develop your skills.

The four skateboards illustrated here are typical of the price ranges described in the text. 1 An expensive skateboard of fibreglass and wood laminate. 2 A cheap plywood skateboard. 3 A polypropylene board. 4 An attractive laminated fibreglass board with a camber.

2
SIMS
PURE JUICE
4

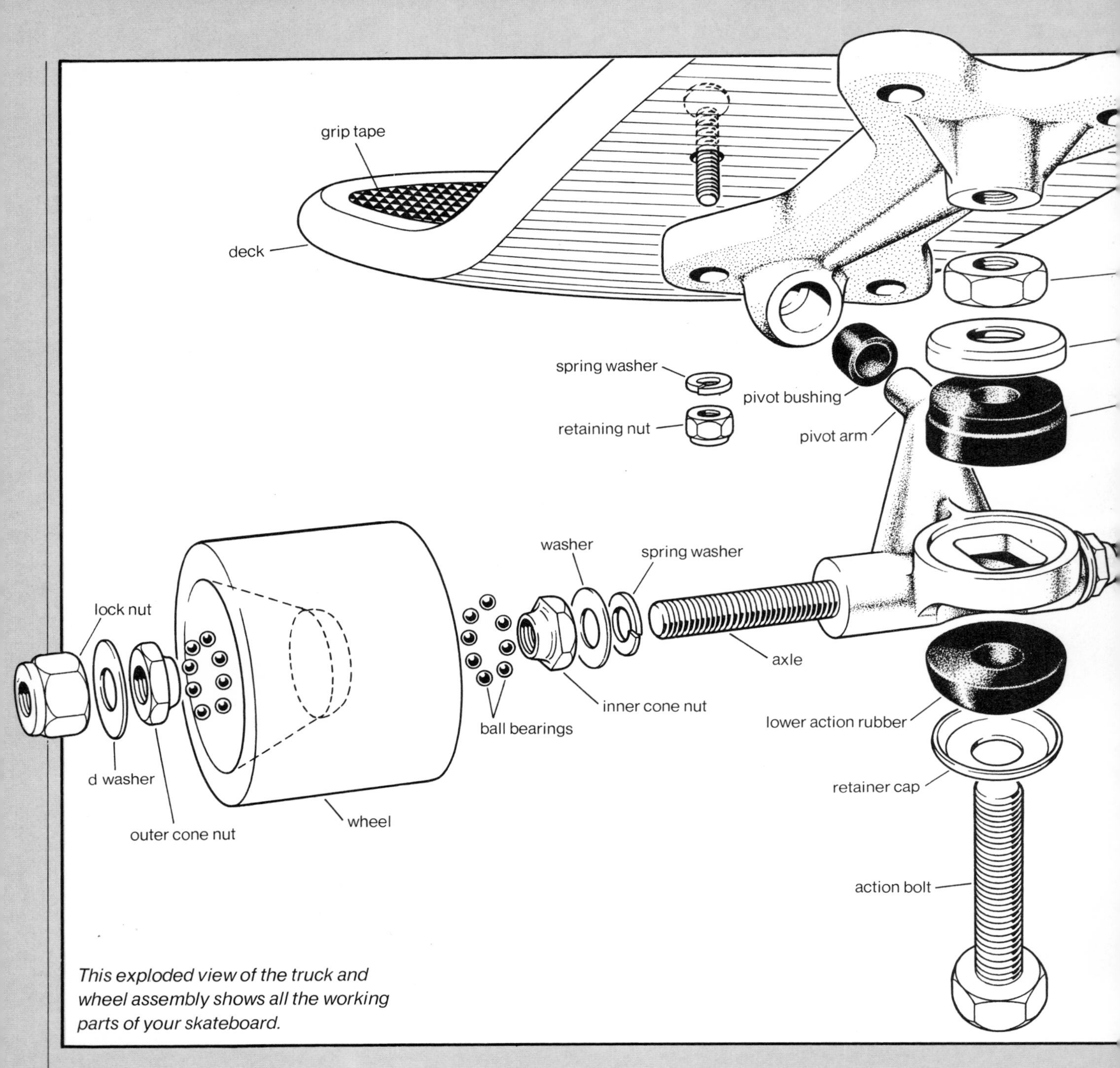

This exploded view of the truck and wheel assembly shows all the working parts of your skateboard.

Maintenance

Skateboards are like motor cars, cycles or any other mechanical means of propulsion – they need maintenance. If they are not maintained properly, they will lose some of their performance. More importantly, as with motor cars, if one part becomes so faulty that it ceases to function while you are travelling, you could be in a dangerous situation. So keep your skateboard in good condition; it will save you money and make you a better skateboarder.

Dismantling

First of all, get yourself some tools which will enable you to dismantle your skateboard. Your skateboard supplier will advise you on the tools needed for your particular model. You might be able to get a tool which will fit several parts of the board.

We will start by describing a complete maintenance, and this will help you to get to know the parts of your skateboard. First, if it is not riveted, remove the base plate from the deck. Then remove the truck from the base plate by loosening the action bolt and nut. Do not unscrew the action nut completely – keep it on the end of the action bolt.

The wheels can now be removed from the axle. If loose bearings are fitted undo the lock nut, taking off the D washer and

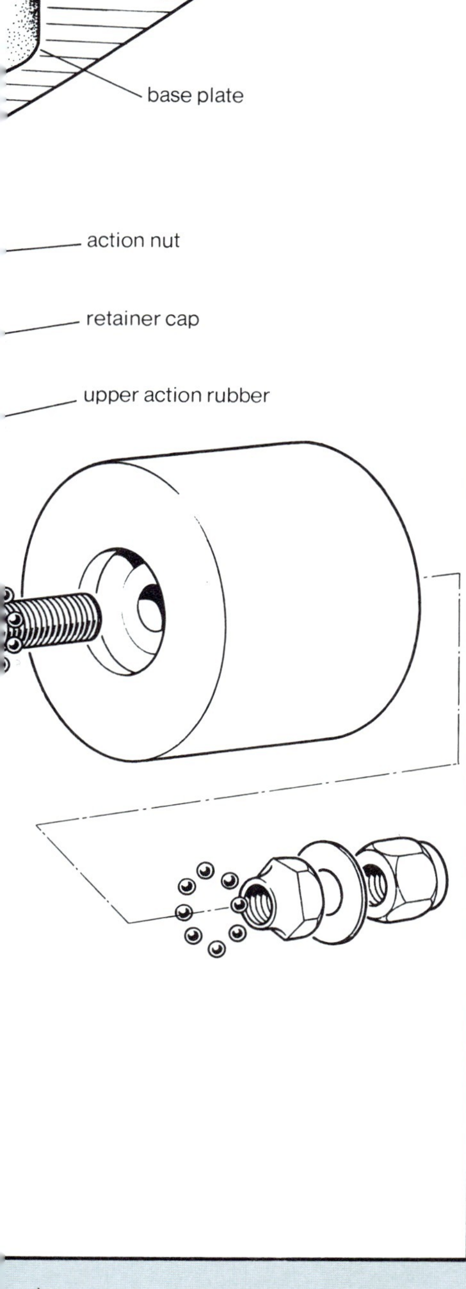

undoing the cone nut. You must take care when removing the wheels not to lose the bearings. You can perform the operation on some sheets of newspaper or a duster to catch the bearings. Precision bearings can be levered out of the wheel complete. You can now unscrew the action nut completely and withdraw the action bolt through the cushions. You have now dismantled your skateboard and can begin examining each part in turn.

Cleaning and checking

If you have loose bearings, first clean the bearings by washing them in paraffin. Roll each separately in a dry rag. Clean the races in which the bearings run with a rag, to remove all dirt. You can do this by wrapping the rag round your finger or round a screwdriver. Cleaning fluids will attack polyurethane wheels, so remove all dirt with paraffin.

Check the action rubbers for deformities and splits. Keep them well away from oil, which will damage them. If there are any splits, buy new action rubbers. Check the retainer caps and replace a cap which is bent with a new one. Check the action bolt and reject it if there are any faults in the threads or if it is bent. Clean the pivot arm and bushing.

Check the wheels for wear. Even polyurethane wheels will show a little wear eventually, usually on the outside, and changing them around with each maintenance will keep the wear even. Polyurethane wheels last a long time and wear will be very gradual. If there is very noticeable wear between one full maintenance and another check the axles very carefully. Check that all nuts and washers are in good condition, and that the threads on the nuts are intact. Clean them all with a dry rag. We have not mentioned precision bearings, because they require little maintenance. Wear is negligible. Dirt accumulation might build up with partially sealed bearings and impair performance, in which case you must clean in paraffin, oil lightly and replace in the wheel.

Examine your deck for splits or cracks, and replace it if it is damaged. Chips on the edge of the deck are to be expected with normal use, and these should be sanded down to avoid splinters. Dents on fibreglass or wood decks should be smoothed out with coarse, then fine, sandpaper.

Reassembling

Now, having inspected and cleaned all parts of your skateboard, and satisfied yourself that each part is in good condition, you are ready to replace the wheels. To replace loose bearings, first put the wheel back on the axle and replace the cone nut, D washer and lock nut, without fully tightening them. With the wheel resting on your newspapers or duster, hold it down and raise the truck by the pivot arm, so that you can drop in the bearings one at a time, and make sure that they are evenly spaced. Bearings can be oiled sparingly with light, general purpose oil. Lower the truck and, keeping the wheel still, spin the truck to ensure that the bearings are seated properly.

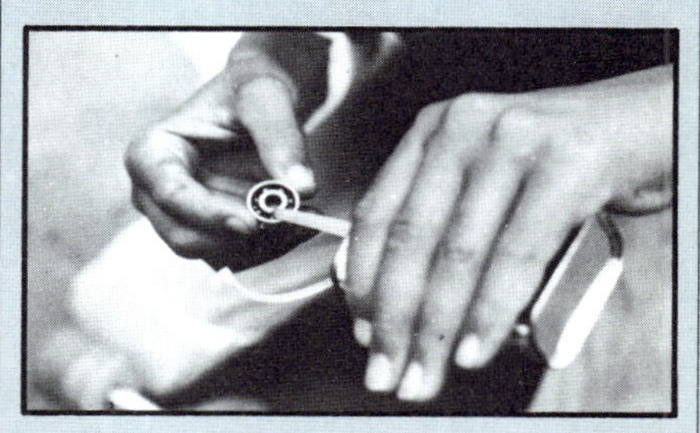

Lightly oil bearings.

Taking the truck and wheel in one hand, drop in the outside bearings and tighten the cone nut until it is clearly too tight. Then loosen it slightly by stages, spinning the wheel each time until you are satisfied that the wheel spins evenly (it should wobble slightly). Then hold the cone nut in place and tighten the lock nut.

When you have fitted all four wheels reassemble the retainer caps and action rubbers on the action bolt. Make sure that a sufficient amount of the action bolt thread goes into the base plate to prevent the thread slipping, and make sure that the action nut is always tight against the base plate. Mount the trucks to the deck, making sure that all nuts are tight.

The precision bearings shown by the removal of a wheel. Note the spacing collar.

Top Checking the tightness and condition of the locknuts.
Centre Checking that the nuts and bolts securing the base plate are tight.
Bottom Checking the tightness of the action nut against the base plate.

When to carry out maintenance

How often should you carry out the above maintenance? This of course depends on how much you use your skateboard. You should examine your board every time you intend to use it and carry out the full maintenance if the wheels aren't running smoothly or if it is particularly dirty. It is easy to overdo the dismantling and reassembling; remember that every time you undo a nut and bolt, you weaken it slightly.

A loose wheel adjustment might cause a loss of a bearing or bearings, and this you might detect by a wobble in the board. A lost bearing will cause additional wear on the other bearings, and increase the chance that more bearings will be lost. You will not be able to persuade a manufacturer that his equipment is faulty if you lose bearings because of loose wheel adjustment. Lost bearings must be replaced at once.

Every time that you intend to go skateboarding, you should make the following checks.

1 Make sure that the lock nuts are fitted and are in good condition.
2 If the base plate is not riveted to the deck, check that the nuts and bolts securing it to the deck are tight.
3 Check that your action rubbers are in good condition. Worn action rubbers must be replaced immediately.
4 Make sure the action nut is tight against the base plate.
5 Check that there are no splinters or splits in the deck.

Make this check every time you return from skateboarding, too. If you get into the habit of always checking your board you will discover any fault which might develop the easy way. Better for you to do some routine maintenance on your skateboard than have somebody perform some running repairs on you.

Safety first

The question of safety is one which should always be at the front of the skateboarder's mind. Any sport involving speed and balance is potentially dangerous, and the top sportsmen accept this and take precautions. Riders in motor cycle Grands Prix are sometimes thought to be among the most skilful and brave sportsmen, but you will not find one who does not think deeply about safety, and you will not find one who rides without his safety clothing, or who takes a chance with the equipment on his racing machine. Take a lesson from the world's best. Ignoring safety precautions is not being courageous, it is being very foolish.

It is a good idea to ask yourself the following questions every time you plan to go skateboarding:

1 Is the place I am going to skateboard a safe place?
2 Am I wearing adequate clothing and safety equipment?
3 Have I checked my skateboard to see that it is safe?
4 Am I going skateboarding with a responsible companion and a responsible attitude?
5 Am I prepared to accept my limitations and not try any tricks that are at present beyond me?
6 If I should fall, do I know how to fall without hurting myself too badly?
7 If there is an accident to my companion, do I know how to cope?

Let us look at these seven questions more closely. As it will add to your pleasure if you can find a good place for skateboarding, it obviously pays to search for such a place rather than to use the first promising spot you come across. If you live near a skateboard park, then your problem is solved, but you are more likely to find a skateboard park if you live in America than elsewhere in the world, where parks are as yet not as numerous as we would like. Otherwise you have to find a spot where there is no motor traffic or pedestrians. A large asphalt or concrete space is best, such as you might find on a recreation ground, or a school playground after hours (don't forget to get the headmaster's permission), or a car park which is empty at weekends. If you have to use public paths, try to find a footpath wide enough for you to turn, and one with a grass verge to help you stop in an emergency. Use these paths only when there are no pedestrians about. If a pedestrian appears while you are skating, stop. He has right of way. Be particularly careful not to skateboard in the presence of old people, who might regard you as a danger. You could easily frighten an old person who might not be able to get out of your way. Never skateboard on the road or any pavements adjacent to the road, where, apart from the chance of meeting pedestrians, a fall might throw you onto the road, with serious consequences.

Examine the surface and the gradient *before* you commence. A gentle slope which meets level ground is ideal, but remember that a long slope, even if it is gentle, is enough to get you moving at a speed which you might find beyond you, especially if you are a beginner. And a long slope with nowhere to go at the bottom can be very dangerous for a learner. A shopping precinct on a Sunday is not a bad place, providing it is large, empty and that there are no plate glass windows to run into. An out-of-control skateboarder hitting one of these will do himself a very nasty injury and land his father with a very expensive bill for repairs.

Clothing is very important. On this page is a picture of a well kitted-out skateboarder. Elegance is not the object; safety is. A

Helmet *A specially designed lightweight helmet with padding and ventilation and a chin cup for comfort and protection is best.*

Long sleeves *Sliding on concrete can take the skin off arms, but long sleeves will prevent a good deal of grazing.*

Gloves *It is natural when falling to put out the hands, which might be badly grazed unless strong gloves, preferably specially designed, are worn.*

Skateboard *The skateboard should be regularly inspected and maintained as described in the section on maintenance.*

Elbow pads *The commonest serious injury is a fracture of the humerus or 'funny bone'. Pads strapped securely round the arms are essential.*

Jeans or trousers *As with long sleeves, a covering for the legs will prevent many unpleasant grazings and cuts.*

Knee pads *Knees are almost as vulnerable as elbows, and pads strapped over the knees will reduce the risk of injury.*

Plimsolls *The ideal footwear gives grip on the skateboard. Rubber soled plimsolls or training shoes are best. Shoes with heels are out.*

helmet is essential. Buy one when you buy your skateboard. Ideally, it should be strong and light. A motorcyclist's helmet is too heavy for comfort. Make sure your helmet fits well and has a strap to go under the chin, or preferably a chin cup for protection and comfort. If it is well padded and ventilated, so much the better.

After your head, the parts of your body most in need of protection are hands and wrists (since you will automatically stick out your arms if you fall), your elbows, your knees and your ankles. Wear good strong gloves, preferably manufactured for the purpose – not dad's Sunday afternoon driving gloves. Wear long sleeves and long trousers. Very bad grazes result from scraping arms and legs on concrete. A denim jacket is fine for the top part of your body – a long-sleeved shirt or sweater is the minimum requirement. Do not skateboard in shorts. Jeans are much better. A track suit (top and bottom) is sensible wear. Always wear elbow and knee pads. You should be able to buy these at any skateboard shop. Never skateboard in bare feet or use shoes with heels. Trainers or plimsolls with rubber soles to give a good grip of the deck are necessary.

Make sure that your skateboard is well maintained and that the bolts holding the wheels to the truck and the truck to the deck are properly tightened. The section on maintenance will give a fuller description of how your skateboard should be maintained.

Skateboard with a companion you can trust. A young beginner should always be supervised and, as even an experienced skateboarder can have an accident, skateboarding should be done in pairs, so that help is always at hand.

All skateboarders want to improve and learn new tricks, or be able to go faster. Indeed, there

is no fun in it unless you are going to get better and better. But do not try to do everything at once. Learn by stages, and perfect one technique before trying the next. Pay no attention to the 'dares' of your friends. Skateboarding is new – there is no need to try to be world champion in your first year. More and more people are taking to skateboarding. You are in at the beginning of the sport and one day you will be one of the best in your area. Just take it steadily – there's no need to rush.

It is a very rare (or untruthful) skateboarder who can say he never fell off. You will not anticipate falling, but when that moment comes, and you are riding on air, it will be too late to

Left A nasty spill. You must expect an occasional accident when you try the difficult manoeuvres, and you'll be glad you were wearing your safety clothing. *Below left* The stages in a rolling fall. When falling forwards go into a forward roll and keep yourself loose. Try to keep your head from hitting the ground.

learn how to fall. Learn it now, and it will do no harm to practise falling on grass or a mat, so that you are prepared. When you are about to fall, or are just beginning to fall, there is always a split second in which you realize your predicament and can take action. Your first object will be to lessen the impact of your fall by lowering your centre of gravity. Therefore you should crouch. The second action should be to loosen your limbs in an effort to be flexible. You must try to land on the more 'padded' parts of the body like your thighs, and you should roll on impact to distribute the force over as many parts of your body as possible. If you do not roll you might slide, which will graze your

When falling to one side spread the impact by rolling, so that no single part of your body takes all the force.

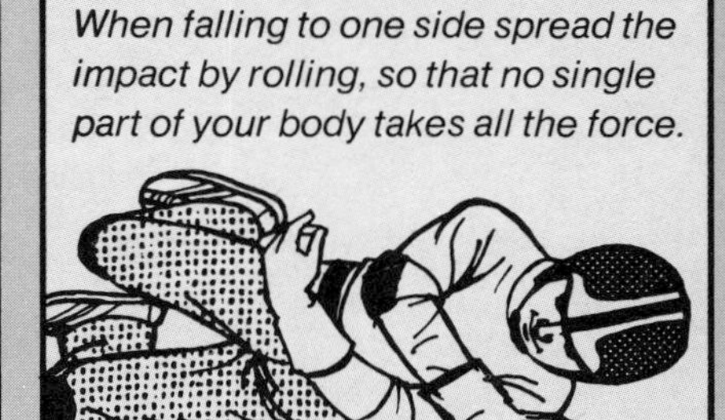

body. If you fall to the right, roll to the right. Use your arms to protect your head. Study the illustrations on falling and practise rolling on grass. Before we look at what to do in case of accident, a couple of other tips will prove useful.

Carry your skateboard to the place where you are going to enjoy your sport. Do not ride through the streets. If you obtain a bag to carry your board, you will also be able to carry some basic first aid equipment as well as your helmet and your knee and elbow pads. If you cycle, make sure your skateboard is firmly attached to the bike, preferably tied along the cross-bar.

Never skate when it is wet. Polyurethane wheels have poor traction on a wet surface, and skateboarding after rain is inviting a spill. Do not skate in the dark. Cats can see in the dark, and moreover have nine lives. You do not enjoy either of these advantages. Do not allow yourself to be pulled along by a cyclist or anybody else. These last tips might seem obvious, but if they deter only one skateboarder from risking it then they are worth including in this book.

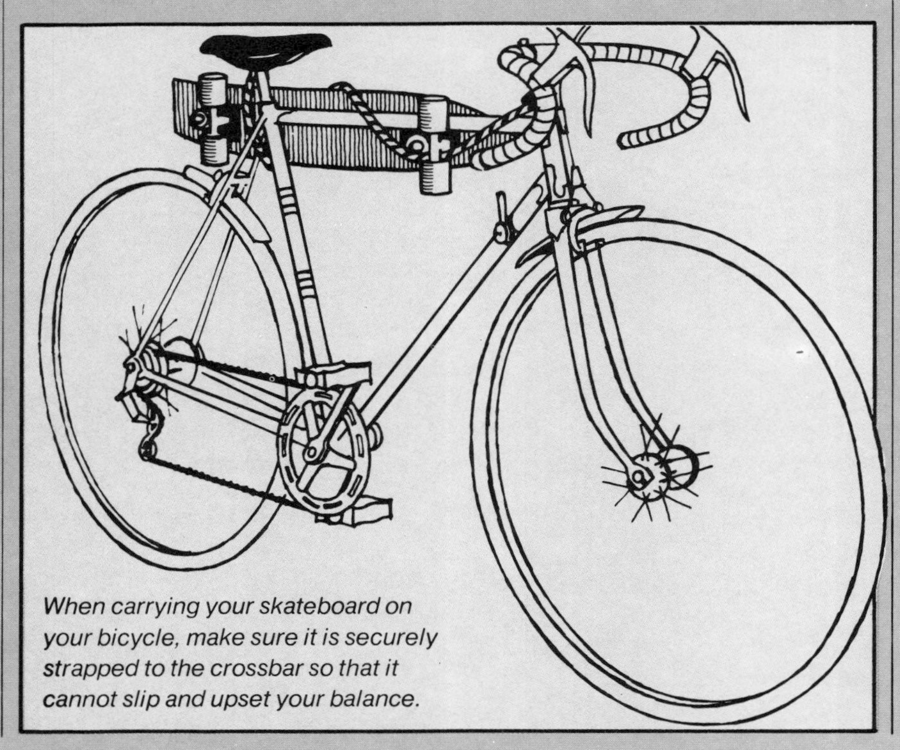

When carrying your skateboard on your bicycle, make sure it is securely strapped to the crossbar so that it cannot slip and upset your balance.

In case of accident

If you encounter an accident while skateboarding you should not attempt first aid unless you have studied the subject and are competent to deal with the patient. Nevertheless there are a few things you can do to help the patient.

1 If he is unconscious, make sure the patient does not choke. It is easy for an unconscious person to swallow vomit, saliva, etc which will choke him. So clear the mouth of any obstructions with your fingers. It is unpleasant but it might save his life. Then turn his head to one side so that if he should vomit the vomit will drain out. Keep watching his breathing to make sure he does not begin to

choke. If he recovers consciousness do not give him anything to drink, eat or smoke.

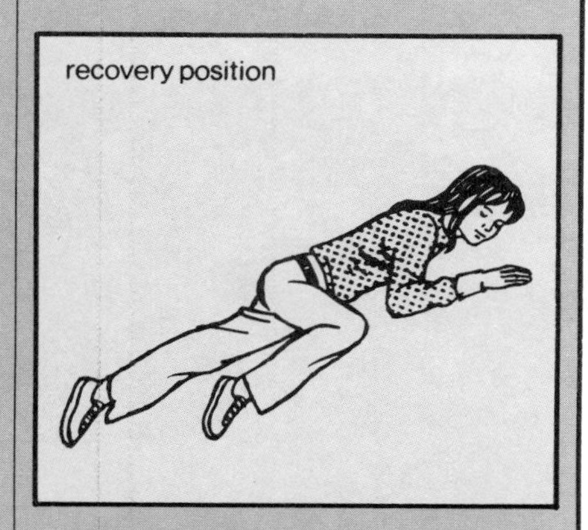

2 Do not move the patient unless it is really necessary, or unless it is dangerous to leave him where he is.
3 Take action to prevent further accidents, such as telling other skateboarders to stop until the patient has been removed to safety.
4 Send somebody for an ambulance.
5 Reassure the patient that you can look after him until professional help arrives.
6 Stay with the patient until help arrives.
7 Tell police or ambulance men all you can about the patient and the accident.
8 Try to keep calm yourself.

Even if you yourself cannot provide first aid there might be somebody else present who can, so you could perform a valuable service by having some first aid equipment with you. It would not take much effort to collect some simple items and to carry them with you when you go skateboarding. Keep them in a metal or plastic box and if you carry your skateboard in a bag keep the first aid box in the bag too. Useful items to carry are perforated absorbent dressings, some plain bandages, some wide cotton crèpe bandage, a large triangular bandage which could be used to make a sling, some safety pins, and some scissors.

The British Safety Council has issued a 12-point safety code for the benefit of skateboarders. These are not points hastily conjured up out of thin air, but instructions which the British Safety Council, after much consideration, believes all skateboarders should follow. Most of them have already been enlarged upon in this section, but safety is so important for skateboarders that we make no apologies for reprinting them here.

1 Do not let children under eight years old skateboard unsupervised.
2 Use a properly manufactured skateboard and check it daily. Do not try and make your own, as this can be very dangerous.
3 Wear proper clothing: helmets, old gloves, and something to protect the elbows and knees. Flat-soled shoes with a good grip should always be worn.
4 Never skateboard on roads and pavements.
5 Select a suitable area to skateboard, in a park or a playground where you do not come into contact with pedestrians.
6 Do not skateboard alone, especially when learning.
7 Learn to skateboard on a very gentle, smooth slope, preferably with a proficient skateboarder.
8 Never run or jump onto a skateboard.
9 When you encounter difficulties – don't hang on until you fall. Step off and start again. Too much too soon can result in a tumble.
10 Form yourselves into clubs and local associations to help each other.
11 Be good ambassadors of your sport. Prove to others that it can be done safely.
12 Remember there is danger in every sport. A responsible attitude in skateboarding will prevent accidents to yourself and others.

The overall winner of a skateboard competition in Britain.

Moving off

We hope you have read patiently the earlier sections of this book and now you want to get out and start skateboarding.

There's one thing you can do even before you leave your home. Just practise standing for a time on the skateboard while it is stationary on your carpet or lawn. Stand with your feet at an angle of forty-five degrees to the way the board is facing with the front foot just behind the front wheels and the rear foot just in front of the back wheels. Which foot is the front foot is for you to decide. Imagine you are actually going along. Which way seems more natural for you – with the left foot leading or the right? Generally, right-handed people, and those who kick a football with their right foot, will prefer to lead with their left foot.

When your feet have got the feel of the board, see what happens when you move around. Shift your weight, and tip the board from side to side. It is not easy to stay on, is it? Bend your knees a little and you will find it easier to tip the board and stay on. Once you are accustomed to standing on the skateboard, there is little to delay any further your first ride. Make sure you've read the section on safety, and run through the check-list to make sure that you are equipped in every way to begin. All right, you have all the correct clothing, everything is fine – let's go.

Carry your skateboard safely to the place you mean to learn. Put on your pads, helmet and gloves and at last you can begin in earnest.

When skateboarding with a friend (as you always should) you can help each other with your gear and check that each other's gear is properly fastened.

The moment when you begin an exciting partnership with your skateboard. Pushing off on your first attempt.

Your first task: choosing a flat surface in a safe place where you can come to no harm and cause no anxiety to others.

The first run

Make your first trials on a flat surface, the larger the better. The first thing to do is to scoot along with one foot on the skateboard and the other providing the push off the ground. This is sometimes called shunting. Put your lead foot on the deck with your toes level with the front wheels, and scoot along. The foot on the board should be pointing straight ahead, not diagonally as it will be when you are skateboarding properly. Your body is therefore facing the front making it easier for you to scoot with your free leg. If you lead with your left leg, then of course your right leg is pushing the ground to the right of the skateboard. When you can do this while keeping the skateboard under control, try doing it the other way round, with your back foot just ahead of the rear wheels while you scoot with what will be your lead foot.

All this will seem elementary. You will soon get tired of it, and you might think it a waste of time, but it is true of all sports that if you learn all the basics thoroughly before going on to the next step, then each succeeding move becomes easier, because you do the simpler things instinctively.

The next step is to get both feet on the skateboard while moving. To do this, begin by scooting as described above and, when you are travelling, put your scooting leg onto the board. Some people prefer to do this by placing their lead foot on the board and bringing their back foot on second. Other people prefer to do it the other way round. Since you are going to learn thoroughly, and will want to be able to do everything, you should practise it both ways.

Let us run through the whole procedure, as it would be if you start with your left foot leading. Place your left foot on the board, pointing forwards with your toe level with the front wheels. Push off with your right foot and, when moving, bring your right foot onto the board just in advance of the rear wheels at an angle of forty-five degrees to the board. In other words, if the board is pointing to 12 o'clock your back

Starting off. 1 Place the rear foot over the rear wheels.

2 Begin moving by pushing off with the free leg.

foot will be pointing half-way between 1 and 2 o'clock. While travelling, you will then need to swivel the lead foot so that it is parallel with the back foot. Your whole body is now pointing the way of your feet, with your left shoulder pointing between 10 and 11 o'clock.

What do you do with your body? You gently bend your knees slightly, with your body relaxed and comfortable, with your bottom stuck out slightly and your trunk inclining slightly forward with your arms slightly in front of you. You are now skateboarding! You lean forward from the waist because the skateboard is easier to control that way. If you lean backwards, the skateboard might slip from under you, and a backward fall is more dangerous than a forward fall.

You are still on a flat surface, so you should not be going at an alarming speed. The next thing you must learn is how to step off the skateboard. If you've ever stepped off a bus just as it is pulling up, or stepped off a roundabout at a fairground, you will understand the principle. You must step off so that you are facing the way you are travelling, because your impetus is going to keep you going in the same direction. So as your foot touches the ground you take off the other and you start running. If you try to stand still you will fall flat on your face, which is not only painful but extremely humiliating! Step off properly and you will be running beside your skateboard.

This has an obvious advantage – you can remain in control of your board and stop it. A runaway skateboard can be painful if it catches you round the ankles. If your free-running skateboard catches somebody else round the ankles the consequences might be even more painful. Keep practising on a flat surface and practise stepping off your skateboard until you are proficient at these manoeuvres before going on to the next.

The correct position for the feet when moving.

3 Accelerate by scooting harder with the free leg.

4 Now bring the scooting leg onto the skateboard.

5 You are now skateboarding for the first time.

Turning

Suppose you are running out of ground, how do you stop without stepping off? You stop by turning and going back the way you came until your momentum is exhausted. Of course, later on, when you are skateboarding on slopes, you stop by turning back uphill, and when you are a little more proficient you can execute a kick turn, but on these first runs on a level surface, you should stop by turning and turning until you stop naturally.

Steering on a skateboard is effected by leaning. If you lean to the right, so that more of your weight is on the right hand wheels, these wheels will turn inwards towards each other and the board will turn to the right. If you lean the other way, the board will turn to the left. The more weight you transfer to one side of the board, the sharper will be the turn, although it will never be more than gentle.

An outside turn, executed by leaning slightly outwards.

An inside turn, executed by leaning slightly inwards.

Practise an inside turn first. An inside turn is a turn to the right if your lead foot is the left. Since you are facing slightly to the right as you stand on your skateboard, you can imagine a continuous turn will take you round in a circle, and all the time you will be facing inside the circle. The inside turn is easier than an outside turn, and it is the best to start with, as should you overdo the weight transference and fall you will fall the way you are facing.

As with all other stages of learning, perfect your steering before you go on to the next. When you can get on, get off, travel confidently on a flat surface and steer to left and right, you are ready to try your skill on a slope.

Downhill skateboarding

After skateboarding on flat surfaces, the next stage is learning how to skateboard downhill. When you get to the skating ground, your first job is to pick your slope. This is important. If on your first try you find yourself going down a hill at the fastest speed you've ever reached, you will not want to start panicking about how to stop or what happens when you arrive at something solid at the bottom. So choose a very gentle not-too-long slope with somewhere suitable to go at the bottom. This might be a gentle uphill slope or a long, flat surface, and preferably bordered by grass rather than iron railings, a ditch or something else equally uncomfortable.

Begin your run by pushing off in the way you do on a flat surface. Make your first run or two standing on your board as you did then. Look ahead, not down at the board. Once you are used to going downhill and know exactly how you can end your run at the bottom of the slope, you can learn more about balance by changing your centre of gravity. Keep relaxed, with your hands slightly in front of you. You can then begin to crouch, by bending your knees more and pushing your hands further forward. Keep your weight evenly distributed, or you will veer to left or right, as you've already discovered. Do not flap your arms about – this will destroy your balance.

Notice the effect of crouching. You have lowered your centre of gravity and decreased the resistance of the air. In a way you have streamlined yourself. You should notice an increased speed. You are now nearer the ground, and if you looked down at the concrete or asphalt rushing by (relatively speaking – you've

Above Skateboarding downhill.
1 The skateboarder begins by standing.
2 She is now crouching slightly, reducing her centre of gravity.
3 She stands again before the slope ends. Right A good technique.

probably travelled faster on a bicycle) you might get alarmed. Just look ahead and concentrate on your balance. If you fall while crouching, you have less time to go into your roll, but on the other hand you have less distance to fall.

When you near the bottom of the slope return from your crouch to the more upright standing position. Downhill skating is a distinct step from skating on the level, so take it steadily. Do it little-by-little on a gentle slope at first, and build up your confidence gradually.

Slalom techniques

By now you can skate down a slope, stand and crouch, and can steer by making left and right turns. When you have practised turning on a slope, you are ready to attempt a slalom.

A skateboard slalom is like a ski slalom. In skiing, the skiers weave between flags stuck in the snow. In skateboarding competitions, cones are used, like those placed by workers around holes or obstructions in the road to keep inquisitive cars at bay.

If you start to practise private slaloms you will have to improvise for cones. Milk bottles and beer bottles are out. Coke and beer cans are better because they lack sharp edges and roll away when hit. Better still are plastic skittles of the type found in children's games. Your first slalom attempt might be with chalk marks on the 'course' – you will not collide with any solid bodies then.

The object of a slalom competition is to cover the course in as short a time as possible without hitting any of the obstacles. Slalom involves speed and manoeuvrability, so we will now learn how to be more efficient at turning and how to increase and decrease speed in turns.

Efficient turns are effected by your hips and trunk. Keeping your knees slightly bent and your weight slightly forward, lean your hips and trunk to the side of your intended turn, tucking your elbows into your waist. A beginner's fault is to turn the shoulders in the direction of turn, which upsets balance. It is easy for an onlooker to see that it is wrong, but it is a natural thing for a beginner to do, and must be resisted.

Maximum speed in a slalom is achieved by weighting and unweighting, much like a motor-racing driver braking and unbraking into and out of a corner. Increasing the weight on the front foot as you approach the obstacle and unweighting as you come out of the turn will get you round each obstacle quicker and in a position to tackle the next.

Traversing a slalom course is fun in itself and need not be a competition, although you may like to keep trying the same slalom course and see if you can improve your time. All the time you are having fun on the slalom you are improving your balance and control.

The slalom. Below The skateboarder coming into a right-hand turn. Bottom A left-hand turn. Left The conclusion of the slalom.

Super skateboarding

This part of the book is called 'Super skateboarding' although it might equally have been called free-style riding. When an ice-skater can skate competently he or she might try figure skating. Although a free-style skater might not call his elaborate figures 'tricks', he is nonetheless always exploring the possibilities of new manoeuvres. A skateboarder can express himself in the same way. It would be too much to expect a spin as rapid as an ice-skater, but he *can* do a spin and there are many other tricky moves he can make. Like ice-skating figures, some skateboard manoeuvres have become standard, and the skateboarder can try these before he starts inventing tricks for himself.

Kick turn

A kick turn is the first technique to master once you are adept at travelling and steering. It is a most useful manoeuvre because it enables you to turn at right angles in either direction. It is therefore useful in avoiding unforeseen obstacles like cats and dogs which rush in front of you. In effect, it enables you to change direction on the spot.

A kick turn can be tried first on a stationary board. Place your back foot behind the rear wheels, right on the tail of the deck, with your front foot in its normal position. Put your weight on your back foot, taking almost all your weight from the front foot so that the front wheels rise off the ground. As they rise, twist the board through 90 degrees, in the direction which you are facing. You do this with your body, not your foot. Get the power from your hips – the front foot merely guides the board.

The above kick turn is called a *push kick turn*. It turns the skateboard in the same direction as the inside turn described in the section on steering. In other words, if your toes point to the right of the skateboard, and you turn to the right, this is a push kick turn. When you have mastered it, try the *pull kick turn*, in which the board turns 90 degrees in the opposite direction. Do this by rotating your body in the same manner as before. Just as an outside turn was found more difficult to achieve than an inside turn, so a pull kick turn is more difficult than a push kick turn.

The next step is obvious. Having mastered the technique of a kick turn on a stationary skateboard, you must now go out and practise it on a moving skateboard. Try it at gentle speeds at first and gradually build up your skill until you can execute a kick turn in either direction.

A kick-tail facilitates kick turns as it helps you to position your back foot correctly while moving. You can use a kick turn for progress on a level surface by a series of partial kick turns in alternate directions, turning the board not 90 degrees but about 30 degrees. This is called *tic-tac* or *click-clacking*, and you will find the board edges forward.

180 degree spin

The name explains the manoeuvre. The 180 degree spin is performed like a kick turn which goes further and turns the board right round until it is pointing in the opposite direction to the original one. It takes more power from your body to turn the board

Performing a kick turn. The large picture shows the front wheels off the ground as the skateboarder puts his weight on the rear wheels. The smaller picture shows the skateboarder turning the board through 90 degrees.

Endover

Sometimes called a *ro-lo*, an endover is a succession of 180 degree spins performed alternatively on the back wheels and the front wheels. The effect is to move the skateboard along in a straight line in one direction. Begin with a stationary skateboard. Place one foot on each end of the deck and perform a 180 degree spin on the back wheels. Then comes a new manoeuvre because you must now perform a 180 degree spin on the front wheels. However, when you consider it, all you have to do is regard the front of the skateboard as the back – the turn itself is exactly the same. With each turn you face in alternate directions, but your skateboard proceeds in a straight line. This manoeuvre, for obvious reasons, is also called a *nose-to-tail 180*.

Above and right A 180 degree spin. The skateboarder begins facing one way, raises the front wheels, and by swivelling his body turns the board through 180 degrees to finish facing the opposite direction.

through 180 degrees. Practise it stationary and then moving on the flat. A good kick-tail deck is useful for this trick, as you will have to push your foot very hard on the back of the board, keeping the front wheels up long enough to swing your body and the board right round.

When you are proficient you can find a downhill slope which runs into an uphill slope (imagine a saucer) so that you can skateboard downhill, up the opposite slope, execute a 180 degree spin and return downhill to go up the first slope again, repeating the manoeuvre and going backwards and forwards, up and down, for as long as you like.

1 In this endover, the skateboarder first raises the rear wheels.

2 He swivels, bringing the rear wheels round in a 180 degree spin.

3 He has completed the first spin.

4 He now puts his weight on the rear wheels, raising the front wheels.

5 He brings the front wheels round in a 180 degree spin.

6 Back in the original position, having moved forward two board lengths.

Below A 360 degree spin. 1 Facing away from us, the skateboarder works up his energy. 2 Halfway through the spin, now facing towards us. 3 Finally coming to rest, having completed a full turn.

360 degree spin

You will know what a 360 degree spin is before we tell you. You managed a kick turn, and you found a 180 degree spin a little more difficult. Next you tried an endover. And now you wonder if you'll ever have the skill to turn the skateboard all the way round through 360 degrees so that it resumes its original direction! The only way to find out is to try.

Begin with your back foot right at the end of the deck. Weight down the back wheels and, as the front wheels rise, begin to whip your arms round in the direction of the turn, turning your whole body and bringing the skateboard right round. Try front side and back side 360 degree spins, and when you are good at those on the back wheels, try them on the front wheels. And when you're good at that, try doing several 360 degree spins without getting off the board. And when you're good at that – well, you're doing well.

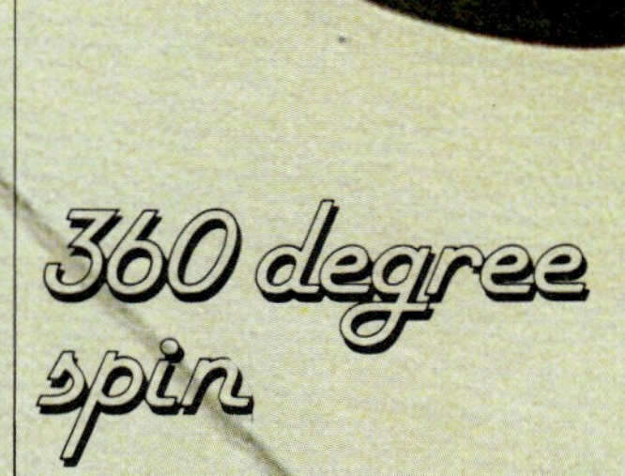

Above The coffin. The skateboarder is skating downhill on his back, feet first.

Coffin

The coffin is explained best by the photograph. Lie on the skateboard like a corpse and away you go, feet first. Do it on a very gentle slope with somewhere to go at the bottom. This is the first trick described where your feet haven't been on the board, and you will find your back doesn't control the board as well. Please be careful. It would be easy to make a joke here about real coffins and real corpses, but by now you will have got the point.

A christie, with the skateboarder holding on to the deck with both hands.

Christie

This trick is also best explained by the photograph. It looks difficult, and it is, requiring excellent balance. Having got moving, position one foot just forward of the centre of the deck, then, crouching down, straighten the other leg out to the front and side, pointing to 2 o'clock. If you extend your right leg, then you must extend your left arm on the other side to balance. Your right hand can grip the deck behind your left foot.

That is one type of christie. It can also be performed with both arms outstretched, or with the straight leg pointing straight ahead and both arms reaching straight out ahead. Balance, as you can imagine, is everything in this trick.

This trick, in any of its variations, will take a lot of practice, and you can expect some spills before you master it. For this trick you should certainly wear gloves, because you will realize that as you practise you will often topple off onto your outstretched hands maintaining, or attempting to maintain, your balance.

When you can do the christie, you can try turns by leaning on the one foot in contact with the deck. A well-performed christie turn is very graceful. When you can do it, call yourself a skateboarder.

The power slide. 1 During a left outside turn, the skateboarder puts his left hand on the ground. 2 Turning his body, and keeping control of the board, he puts his right hand down. 3 He has stopped. 4 He draws the skateboard up beneath him and is ready to skate off again.

Power slide

The power slide is another manoeuvre which will bring home to you the absolute necessity of gloves. You may have seen a speedway rider turn his bike by putting down one leg and using it as a brake and a pivot. In a power slide you use your hands in a similar way. With a moderate speed up, you go into an outside turn, lowering your centre of gravity as you do so. If turning to the right, you place your right hand on the ground first, and twist your upper body round in the direction of the turn to bring your left hand to the ground. You must keep your feet firmly on the skateboard to stop it. Try not to stretch your body too much or you will lose control of the board. When you can do this trick you can try it with your body extended further. And when you're satisfied with your skill at this, try a power slide with one hand.

A power slide is a very effective stop. Alternatively, instead of extending your legs you can draw the board back underneath you and ride off again.

Spinner

This is the first trick where you will actually jump off the skateboard in motion and land on it again. It consists of jumping from the skateboard, spinning your body 360 degrees in the air, and landing on the skateboard again to continue your ride.

A 360 degree spin from the ground is not too easy, and this is one trick you can practise first without a skateboard at all. Then you can practise it on a stationary skateboard. When you get on a moving skateboard, try a 180 degree spin first, spinning your body so that when you land your lead foot becomes your rear foot. Do this trick at a gentle speed, or your skateboard will have moved on too far while you are still in the air.

One tip. You will sometimes find, especially early on, that you realize you are not going to land on the board properly while you are half way through your spin. In this case, open your legs so that you miss the board altogether and land on the ground. But ensure beforehand that your skateboard has somewhere to go, because there is no way you will prevent it going off on a free run.

Above The spinner. 1 The skateboarder jumps and twists 360 degrees. 2 Back on the skateboard in her original position.

A skateboarder walking on his board. The diagrams show two alternative sequences of foot movements.

Walking the board

This manoeuvre is simply walking up and down your deck using the technique shown in the diagram. There is little to describe in this trick. The length of your deck will determine how many steps you can take in either direction before walking back again. You can practise first on a stationary board, but by now you will be so used to your skateboard that you will find this easy. The only other advice we can give is to get out and practise.

BEADLE
BOARD
TEAM

Wheelie

Wheelies are popular tricks where you travel on two wheels only – either front or back. The easiest is the two-foot tail wheelie. Move back along the board until the front wheels leave the ground. The trick now is to keep the board balanced and moving on two wheels. Your legs should be slightly bent, with your arms helping balance by being outstretched, or reaching upwards from the elbows. Your body should be arched, so that your upper body is leaning forward in relation to your thighs. A good kick-tail is useful for a rear wheelie, as you do not want the tail of your deck to scrape the ground while you practise.

The wheelies are performed on one pair of wheels only. The four pictures on these pages show a two-foot nose wheelie, a one-foot nose wheelie, a two-foot rear wheelie, a one-foot rear wheelie.

A nose wheelie is more difficult. Both feet should be on the front of the deck and a kick-nose is useful here. If the nose of your deck touches the ground as you practise a nose wheelie you might damage your toes as well as pitch forward as the board tips.

When you can do both two-foot wheelies you can try one-foot nose and tail wheelies, and when you can perform them on a gentle slope with a suitable getaway at the bottom, you can practise turns.

L-sit and V-sit

These tricks are very difficult to perform and owe something to gymnastics. Perhaps if an Olympic gold medallist took up skateboarding he or she would perform a very good L-sit and V-sit, but many people will perhaps find the degree of balance and strength required beyond them.

The L-sit comes first. It can be practised on the ground first. You need to balance yourself on your hands with your legs straight out in front of you, as in the illustration. If you can do that, you should be able to do it on a stationary skateboard, although the wobble will make it harder. Well done! All you have to do now is try it on the move.

The V-sit, as the illustration shows, is basically the same thing, but now you have to bring your legs up to form an angle like a V with your trunk.

If you master either of these tricks, you can call yourself an exceptional skateboarder, for few can perform them.

The L-sit. Strong arms and good balance are required to achieve this position even on a stationary skateboard.

The V-sit is a progression from the L-sit. The legs are raised to form a V with the trunk.

Handstand

This is another trick which owes something to the gymnasium. If you cannot do a handstand on the ground without a wall to prop your feet against, do not try this one! If you can do a regular handstand, you will want to amaze friends and influence people by performing it on a skateboard. You might find it easier to grasp the ends of the deck rather than place your hands flat upon it. More than ever it is essential to check your equipment and have your helmet and pads on for this trick.

Do the handstand on a level surface or very gentle slope. You will not want to pick up much speed with your head pointing at the ground. You must push the board off as you raise yourself into the handstand position. Even a superb gymnast will not master turning first try, so make sure you have somewhere to go before you start travelling.

You might regard a handstand as halfway through a cartwheel, and this will help you visualize a spectacular stop when performing a handstand on a skateboard. Just complete the cartwheel, keeping hold of the skateboard which finishes raised above your head. Very neat!

Two impressive handstands, one with legs upright and another with legs bent. Another fine handstand is shown on the back cover of the book.

Multiple board tricks

On the next few pages are shown a few manoeuvres with two or more skateboards. It is unlikely that you own two skateboards, so you will need the help of a friend with these tricks. We hope you have followed the safety code and performed all your skateboarding so far with a companion present, so this need not be a drawback.

Bridge

You might know the exercise known as a 'crab', often performed in physical education classes at school. If you are happy in the crab position, you can form a bridge with two skateboards.

Practise first on stationary skateboards, just getting into the position in the illustration. When you are thoroughly at home in the position, try travelling on a gentle slope, one which flattens out and ends in nice soft grass, because it is very difficult to stop in a dignified way when your hands and feet are all controlling boards. Your friend can push you off. It is difficult to turn when travelling in the bridge position, as you have to weight one side of one skateboard with your hands and the corresponding side of the other with your feet. Try it only when you are slowing up on level ground, and expect to find yourself spreadeagled on your back the first few times.

The picture inset left shows a skateboarder forming a stationary bridge on level ground, while another on a third skateboard with the help of a push from a friend, is travelling in the coffin position under the bridge.

Daffy

Pictures of a skateboarder performing a daffy suggest a frogman whose flippers have gone wrong. It is basically a combination of a one-foot nose wheelie on one board, while your free foot is performing a one-foot rear wheelie on another board. It looks impressive, but if you have

The bridge. The skateboarder adopts a crab position, grasping one skateboard with his hands, with his feet on the other. The picture inset left shows three skateboarders using three boards. One skateboarder is making a bridge while another is pushed beneath it in the coffin position.

mastered the one-foot wheelies you will find it is a not-too-difficult progression to the daffy. You begin by positioning one board a few metres ahead of you and skate towards it on the other board. As you near the free board, start a one-foot rear wheelie on the board you're on. When you reach the front board, place your free foot on the nose, raising its tail and performing a one-foot nose wheelie on that board. With a little practise you will find you can travel with both boards under perfect control.

The daffy. Top right The skateboarder, about to place his free foot on the front board. Right Proceeding under control.

Catamaran

Two good skateboarders can build up an understanding and have great fun with a catamaran. Begin together, each of you on your own board, on a gentle slope, one leading with the left foot and the other with the right, so that you are facing each other. Join hands and crouch, and get as close to each other as you can. With practice and understanding you can weld yourself into one unit and, by agreeing beforehand on a code of instructions, you can shout directions to each other and turn as one.

Another trick is for each of you to sit on one skateboard with your feet on the other, again holding hands. You are now really locked together. You can extend this idea and weld together as many of you as you like in the way that trick motor-cyclists at military tattoos can join up and perform all sorts of balancing tricks. But do not be too ambitious. You must understand what you are going to do and practise each move before going on to the next. The pictures on these pages give you some ideas for other tricks to try.

Catamaran shots. 1 In this catamaran, the skateboarders are each sitting on one board with their feet on the other. 2 Two skateboarders lying back with their hands grasping the decks. Notice how necessary elbow pads and helmets are in this manoeuvre. 3 Three skateboarders riding on three boards. 4 Comradeship and team spirit. A progressive catamaran, with six skateboarders on four skateboards. Not to be attempted without careful planning.

Long jump

The sequence of pictures best illustrates the principle of the long jump. One way to perform it is for two or more skateboarders to lie down with a skateboard on its end against the nearest skateboarder's side (wheels pointing outwards unless he likes collecting bruises). Another skateboard is

The long jump. 1 The skateboarder is just hitting the spare skateboard stood on edge against the side of his

placed on the opposite side ready for the long jumper to land on it and carry on skateboarding. The trick is performed on the level, not downhill. The long jumper approaches at a reasonable speed, and as his board hits the one on its side he jumps over the prostrate skateboarders to land on the skateboard on the other side and continue on his way.

If you have performed the long jump at school in athletics you will know that if you concentrate on height you will also achieve length, and the same principle applies to the skateboard long jump. Make sure that your feet land in the correct positions on the free skateboard. If you know you cannot manage this, miss the skateboard altogether and keep running to exhaust your momentum.

first colleague lying down. 2 In mid-air. 3 Landing on the free skateboard ready to skate away.

High jump

The high jump is also shown by the sequence of photographs. This time the board passes underneath your friend who is making an obstacle for you to jump over, and you land on the board after making your jump and continue skateboarding. The skills lie in the take-off and the landing. You must take off without upsetting the direction or speed of your board, and you must land with your feet in the correct positions and perfectly balanced. This is easy to practise because you can make little jumps while travelling on your skateboard without actually jumping over anything, increasing the height gradually until you are confident enough to jump over an obstacle like your friend.

As with the long jump, if you feel you are not going to land correctly on your board, miss it altogether and start running forward to preserve your balance, and catch your skateboard.

The high jump. 1 The skateboarder ready to take off. 2 Jumping over his colleague, while the skateboard continues to run free. 3 Landing on the skateboard and continuing to travel forward.

The future

Skateboarding is here to stay. Two of the areas where we will see development in the future are in the construction of skateparks, and in the organization of competitions. The pictures on these and the following pages give you a glimpse of the pleasures to come.

Skateparks

The best place to skate is in a skatepark specially designed for skateboarders. There are a number in America, but relatively few elsewhere. Skateboarders who practise their sport in the best facilities they can find near home, look with envy at the pictures in magazines showing slick skaters performing intricate manoeuvres in concrete bowls and sculptured race-ways.

Although many of the tricks described in this book are very difficult, and do not come with a week's spasmodic practice, the tricks some of the best skateboarders can perform look almost impossible.

What sort of facilities should the best skateparks offer? The following are already available in America: swimming pool-like bowls in which the skateboarder can rise up the walls to the lip like a wall-of-death rider at a fair ground; pipes with the potential for upside-down riding – an even more sensational death-and-gravity defying trick; huge concrete surfaces; tunnels; long slalom runs like the bobsleigh runs at the winter Olympic Games; mazes; long pipes with interior lighting; and

Left Too keen to go home.
Below Inside a tunnel, a facility that the best skateparks should provide.

Right The large photograph shows a skateboarder actually horizontal as he comes down from the lip. casting the sort of shadow you might see in a horror film. Below More skateparks are needed. These skateboarders await their turn to run down into the bowl. Below right Over the lip. This skateboarder is skilful enough to take two wheels over the edge before turning back.

shops with skateboard equipment and advice, like the professional's shop at a golf course.

How would you like to skateboard down a long ramp which takes you through a tunnel and empties you out into a bowl where you can zoom round the sides until you get tired of this, and then go off to try the slalom run? That is what skateparks can offer and that is what skateboarders in other parts of the world can look forward to if skateboarding takes as big a hold as it has in many parts of America. There is every sign that it will in Britain, where there are already a few parks in operation.

The pictures on these and the following pages are to whet your appetite and show you what skateboarding can become in your part of the world. Who knows, one day soon we might all be going off to the skatepark just as we have in the past gone to the ice-rink, the tennis courts, the putting green and the bowling alley.

Left Riding the rim, a popular manoeuvre among the better skateboarders at the skatepark. *Above* A slick turn from the rim.

Competitions

Skateboard competitions are common in California; in July 1977 the first official British competition was held at Crystal Palace, near London. Competitions are so new that there is as yet no standardization on the events. There are not even established experts who can judge and mark free-style tricks to everybody's satisfaction. But skateboarding is growing so rapidly, and the best skateboarders so want to compete against each other, that it is certain that eventually officially recognized organizing bodies, rules and procedures will emerge.

At present, competitions are usually broken down into age groups and might be broken down into boys' and girls' events. The age divisions might be under 13, 13 to 16, and over 16 but the organizers of the competitions vary in their ideas.

Most competitions will include a free-style event, in which competitors are asked to perform a variety of tricks in a given time, say two minutes, and a group of

Above *Guy Grundy, a leading American skateboarder, during his run at Signal Hill, California, in 1977, which was timed at 80 km per hour (50 mph).* *Right* *Scenes from an American skateboarding competition, showing the high jump and slalom.*

32
MASTERS

judges marks them, figure-skating style. But, of course, competitors will have to make the best of the facilities that are available – if one's best trick is performed on a steep bank, and there isn't one, hard luck.

A slalom event is the easiest to hold. Competitors can make two timed runs, the skateboarder with the best time being the winner. Time penalties are added for knocking over a cone. A downhill race is also easy enough to organize, provided that a long enough slope is available to allow a reasonable difference between the best and worst times. In America, some speed fanatics

Above Enthusiastic spectators photographing a competitor in the American championships. *Left* The free-style event in a British championship at Crystal Palace. Perhaps in future competition organizers will insist on full protective clothing including knee pads. *Above right* A spectacular long jump onto two skateboards. *Below right* A free-style skateboarder in the 14-16 year-old class. *Far right:* A handstand from the British championships.

take such an interest in downhill speed runs that they build streamlined shells round their skateboards in which they lie face down, so that they look like a bobsleigh shooting downhill. At the annual speed run at Signal Hill, California, in 1977, the fastest skateboard, which you would not recognize as a skateboard, as the lying down rider is completely enclosed in a streamlined shell, clocked 92 kilometres per hour (57mph). The fastest skateboarder standing up, adopting a style like a downhill skier, achieved 80 kilometres per hour (50mph).

This is really fast moving, and a long way from a beginner trying a kick turn in the school playground. It shows the range skateboarding has achieved in such a short time. Perhaps, one day, speed, slalom and free-style skateboarding will be events in the Olympic Games, with World, European and Pan-American champions.

These pages show events from competitions, emphasizing that skateboarding, in only a few years, has changed from a pastime to a sport that has gripped the imagination of those who love and perform it.